THE ANTARCTIC

BIOMES

Lynn M. Stone

The Rourke Corporation, Inc.
Vero Beach, Florida 32964

PHOTO CREDITS
All photos © Lynn M. Stone

Library of Congress Cataloging-in-Publication Data
Stone, Lynn M.
    The Antarctic / by Lynn M. Stone.
        p. cm. — (Biomes)
    Includes index.
    Summary: Explores the frozen region which is located at the
bottom of the earth and which consists of the Antarctic continent,
ocean and sea islands.
    ISBN 0-86593-421-5
    1. Ecology—Antarctica—Juvenile literature. 2. Antarctica—
Juvenile literature. [1. Ecology—Antarctica. 2. Antarctica.] I.
Title. II. Series: Stone, Lynn M. Biomes.
QH84.2.S85 1996
574.5'2621—dc20   95-46187
                                      CIP
                                      AC

Printed in the USA

TABLE OF CONTENTS

The Antarctic   5
The Antarctic Ocean   6
Life in the Sea   9
Antarctica   11
Life on Antarctic Lands   14
Antarctic Birds   16
Antarctic Mammals   19
Visiting the Antarctic   20
Protecting Antarctica   22
Glossary   23
Index   24

THE ANTARCTIC

Antarctica is the great white, frozen **continent** (KAHN ti nent) at the bottom of the Earth. The south pole is on Antarctica.

Most of Antarctica is covered by ice and snow. No continent on Earth is higher, colder, or windier.

Icy Antarctica makes the ocean around it cold, too. Each winter huge blocks of ice stretch across the sea from Antarctica's shores.

Together, the Antarctic continent, ocean, and sea islands are called the Antarctic region.

The Antarctic is a region of icy seas, tall mountains, strong winds, and frozen land

THE ANTARCTIC OCEAN

The Antarctic, or Southern, Ocean is cold and deep. It is also rough, except where ice covers its surface. During winter, unbroken sea ice can reach 1,000 miles from the coast of Antarctica.

During the summer break-up of ice, the ocean is full of ice blocks. Some of the largest icebergs could hold cities!

Beneath the ice and waves, the Antarctic Ocean is amazingly rich in animal life.

Floating icebergs bob in the Antarctic Ocean in summer

LIFE IN THE SEA

The Antarctic Ocean supports even the animals that spend part of their lives on land, too. Penguins, for example, nest on shore, but they need the sea for the fish and **krill** (KRIL) they eat.

Krill are shrimplike creatures. Billions of them live in the Antarctic Ocean. Many kinds of large **marine** (muh REEN), or sea, animals eat krill.

Krill and some of the other small marine animals eat **algae** (AL jee). Algae, a plant, grows by changing sunlight into food.

Fed by the sea nearby, a giant petrel goes ashore to nest and raise chicks

ANTARCTICA

Much of Antarctica is covered by a crust of ice more than one mile thick. The ice makes Antarctica the highest continent.

Winter temperatures in Antarctica dip to -120° Fahrenheit. Even summer days on the Antarctic mainland rarely top freezing (32° Fahrenheit). The Antarctic **peninsula** (pe NIN suh luh) and the islands around it are warmer.

The few places where ice and snow melt away in summer are rough and rocky.

Antarctica is the white wilderness at the bottom of the Earth

On islands some distance from the coldest continent,
seals can loaf in wild grasses

Albatrosses sweep over the Antarctic seas on long, pointed wings

LIFE ON ANTARCTIC LANDS

Nearly all the Antarctic continent rests under snow and ice. The few spots of open soil are too rocky, cold, and windy for most plants to survive.

Without many plants, Antarctica cannot support wild land animals, except for a few insects and other small, boneless creatures. Sea birds, such as petrels and penguins, come ashore only to rest, lay eggs, and raise their young. Seals visit the seashores to rest and raise pups.

14

Plants are scarce in the Antarctic, so the gentoo penguin builds its nest of pebbles

ANTARCTIC BIRDS

Thanks to the richness of the Antarctic Ocean, the region is home to millions of sea birds. Most of them are penguins and petrels.

Petrels and their long-winged cousins, the albatrosses, are excellent fliers. They take food from the sea surface.

Penguins don't fly, but they are fine divers. Their wings drive them after underwater **prey** (PRAY).

Penguins stay warm in the icy sea because of a wrap of thick feathers and body fat.

Feathers and fat keep Antarctic penguins warm at sea and in icy air

ANTARCTIC MAMMALS

Millions of seals live in the Antarctic, along with a few thousand whales. You won't find polar bears, though, or any other wild land mammals in the Antarctic region.

Like Antarctic birds, Antarctic mammals depend upon a supply of seafood — fish, krill, squid, and shellfish. The killer whale, or orca, eats seals, penguins, and even other kinds of whales.

Southern elephant seals bake themselves in the summer sun on a shore of the Antarctic peninsula

VISITING THE ANTARCTIC

Antarctica is the only continent without a group of native people. No one is really *from* Antarctica. Every person in the Antarctic is a visitor.

Most visitors travel to the Antarctic between November and February, during the Antarctic summer. Long-distance travel is by ship or plane. Airplanes land on snow runways. There are no long roads or railways.

Some visitors are scientists. Others are people who want to see or study Antarctica's amazing wildlife and scenery.

Antarctic visitors find a dazzling wilderness world of white and blue

PROTECTING ANTARCTICA

Many countries, including the United States and Canada, are working together to protect Antarctica and the entire region. These countries have signed the Antarctic Treaty. They agree to keep building projects and military bases out of Antarctica.

By protecting the region, the world is saving an amazing place and its amazing animals.

People who visit Antarctica today find it wonderfully wild, just as it was eons ago.

Glossary

algae (AL jee) — a group of rootless, nonflowering plants that can live in extreme cold and conditions where many other plants cannot

continent (KAHN ti nent) — a huge piece of land somewhat separated from others by water, mountains, or a narrow strip of land; such as North America, South America, Antarctica

krill (KRIL) — shrimplike animals that live in cold seas

marine (muh REEN) — of or relating to the sea and salt water

peninsula (pe NIN suh luh) — a long, narrow strip of land surrounded on three sides by water

prey (PRAY) — an animal that is killed by another animal for food

INDEX

albatrosses   16
algae   9
animals   6, 9, 14
   marine   9
Antarctica   5, 6, 11,
   14, 20, 22
Antarctic Ocean   6, 9, 16
Antarctic peninsula   11
Antarctic region   5
Antarctic Treaty   22
fish   9, 19
ice   5, 6, 11, 14
insects   14
islands   5, 11
krill   9, 19
mammals   19

penguins   9, 14, 16, 19
people   20
petrels   14, 16
plants   14
sea birds   14, 16
seals   14, 19
snow   5, 11, 14
south pole   5
whales   19
   killer   19